To all the ch
with 6

C000018675

PICKCHEESE, BILLY WISE
AND COBBLE

Illustrated Folk Names of Birds

Steve Palin

Taghan Press
Norfolk

PICKCHEESE, BILLY WISE AND COBBLE

Copyright © Steve Palin 2002

All Rights Reserved

No part of this book may be reproduced in any form,
by photocopying or by any electronic or mechanical means,
including information or retrieval systems,
without permission in writing from both the copyright owner
and the publisher of this book.

ISBN 1-871482-20-8

First Published 2002 by Thomas Lyster Ltd
for TAGHAN PRESS
Oak House, Oak Lane, East Ruston
NORFOLK
NR12 9JG

Printed in Great Britain for Taghan Press

PICKCHEESE, BILLY WISE AND COBBLE

Illustrated Folk Names of Birds

Introduction

In keeping with my two previous books on collective nouns, this book is intended as a celebration of the richness of language and folklore associated with birds, but whilst its subject has inevitable etymological undertones, it is not intended to be an academic or analytic work. The accompanying illustrations create a book that has a different "feel" from other books with similar subject matter and will hopefully introduce a different readership to the provincial names of birds.

Those readers wishing to pursue the philology and etymology of birds' names in a more academic and comprehensive context may find the bibliography at the back of the book helpful. In particular however, Francesca Greenoak's _The Birds of the Air_, C E Hare's _Bird Lore_, Christine Jackson's _British Names of Birds_ and W B Lockwood's _The Oxford Dictionary of British Bird Names_ are well worth a read.

Our currently accepted names for British birds are derived from many other language influences. These include our own original Celtic speech or "Old British"; Latin from the Romans; Anglo-Saxon or Old English (itself of Continental/Germanic influence) from the early invasions of the Angles and Saxons; Norse, from the Viking invasions of the North, and Old French from the Normans. It was not until the times of the Tudors that English began to stabilise into something like the form in which it appears today. Even so, Celtic continued in parts of Scotland, whilst Irish, Scottish and Manx Gaelic still held sway in their respective regions. Welsh, of course was a further maintained regional language and Cornish was spoken until the end of the eighteenth century. These language influences are apparent to a lesser or greater extent across the spectrum of our names for British birds.

Within the wider philological development of the English language, birds' names were constructed from a variety of different perspectives. Some names, such as **Greenshank, Goldeneye** and **Crossbill**, refer to the birds' appearance; others refer to their habits, such as **Wagtail, Oystercatcher** and **Shearwater**. Some names relate to the place in which birds are seen, such as the **Meadow Pipit** or **Brook Runner** (**Water Rail**). Birds such as the **Cuckoo** and **Curlew** are named after the sounds they make. This is also the reason for the quail's other names of **Quick-me-dick** and **Wet-my-lips**, and the **Yellowhammer**'s folk-name of **Bread-and-Cheese** - its call being fully transcribed as "little-bit-of-bread-and-no-cheese".

Some of the most interesting folk-names, however, are derived from legends or local superstitions. That supposed harbinger of storm - the **Mistle Thrush** - became known as **Storm Cock**. The **Storm Petrel** was called **Mother Carey's Chicken** by sailors (Mother Carey being a corruption of Mother Mary), reflecting its supposed and almost divine ability to forewarn of disaster at sea. The **Devil's Bitch** and **Devil Screech** are just two of many rather self-evident derogatory names applied to the **Swift**, its satanic association earned reputedly because of its dusky plumage and its penetrating screeching call.

Today the names of birds continue to be debated, although this is more often to do with scientific classification or the standardisation of names across different countries and continents. (Standardisation was at one time necessary within Britain itself - there are so many examples of the same folk names for entirely different birds!) Modern communication in all of its forms is resulting in the demise of whole languages, let alone any dialect variations within a language. We can only regret that perhaps no-one will ever again refer to the **Whinchat** as **Furze-jack** or the **Goldfinch** as **Thistle-tweaker**, or that the **Long-tailed Tit** will be unable to rejoice in its alternative and more picturesque name of **Bum Barrel**!

AVOCET

BUTTERFLIP

COBBLER'S AWL

yarwhelp

AVOCET

The name **Avocet** is of Italian derivation, originating from *Avosetta*, a name from the Venetian coast where the bird lives. The name *Avosetta* was first recorded in 1603, and subsequently adopted by Linnaeus. In Britain, Thomas Pennant initially called it the **Scooping Avoset** (sic) before standardising it as simply **Avoset** in 1776. The present spelling goes back to 1833.

It is not surprising that many of the **Avocet**'s folk names refer to its distinctive up-turned bill - **Cobbler's Awl** could hardly be the name of another bird. Other names that refer to its bill include **Awl-bird**, **Crooked Bill** and **Scooper**. The avocet's yelping cry when disturbed gives rise to a number of other names. It shares the folk name **Yarwhelp** with the Bar-tailed Godwit, the name **Yaup** with the Curlew, and the name **Yelper** with the Redshank.

The Royal Society for the Protection of Birds' emblem displays the black-and-white plumage of the **Avocet**. This plumage is reflected in the name **Black-and-white Flighter** and also in the name **Picarini**, *pica* being the Magpie genus of birds. The RSPB has been instrumental in the Avocet's remarkable comeback after a century's absence in Britain. It now breeds regularly on the East Coast and indeed has recently extended its range to include the North West of England.

Awl-bird ((Suffolk); Barker; Black-and-white Flighter; Butterflip; Clinker (Norfolk); Cobbler's Awl; Cobbler's Awl Duck; Crooked Bill; Picarini; Scooper; Shoe Awl; Shoeing Horn; Scooping Avocet; Whaup, Yarwhelp, Yaup (Norfolk); Yelper (Lincolnshire)

BARN OWL

JENNY HOWLETT

BILLY WISE

WOOLERT · ROARER

BARN OWL

Surely one of the nation's favourite birds, the **Barn Owl** has been the source of untold numbers of ghost stories. Its habit of frequenting church towers to nest (and therefore frequenting graveyards) gave rise to one of its names - **Church Owl.** In addition its ghostly figure has often been seen in the twilight (when ghosts, as we all know, wake up) and its human-like screech in these places, at these times, has chilled the bones of many a passer-by.

Many of this owl's folk names derive from its appearance: **White Hoolet**, **White Owl**, **Silver Owl**, **Yellow Owl**, or in Gaelic **Cailleach-oidhche Gheal** meaning white woman of the night. Its shrieking call has also given rise to **Screech Owl** (in fact the name of a distinct species), **Scritch Owl**, **Hissing Owl**, **Screaming Owl** and **Roarer**. **Billy Wix**, **Billy Wise** and similar names are basically onomatopoeic, reflecting the rhythm and sound of the Barn Owl's cry.

The Barn Owl has a special place in our hearts though. Farmers in particular have welcomed it as an expert rodent-catcher and often adapted their barns to accommodate it. Some folk names of this bird indicate its familiarity, like **Jenny Owl**, **Madge Howlet**, **Moggy** and **Pudge**.

Owls, like witches and vampires, are creatures of the night and its associated superstitions often reflect this. However, the Barn Owl's human-like countenance with its forward facing eyes, together with its reputation for sagacity provide a balance in our traditional view of this beautiful bird.

Berthuan (Cornwall); Billy Owl; Billy Whit; Billy Wise; Billy Wix; Cailleach-oidhche Gheal; Cherubim (Northamptonshire); Church Owl; Cream Coloured Owl; Deviling (Surrey); European Screech Owl; Gil-hooter, Gill Houter, Gill Howter (Cheshire, Norfolk); Gillihowlet (Scotland); Gilly Owlets, Gilly White [young] (Shropshire); Hissing Owl (Yorkshire); Hobby Owl (Northamptonshire); Hullart, Hullot (Cheshire); Jenny Howlett, Jenny Owl, Jenny Owlen (N England); Madge Howlet; Moggy; Oolert, Owlen, Owlerd (Shropshire); Pudge; Roarer; Scritch Owl; Screech Owl; Silver Owl (Scotland); Stix (Cornwall); Ullat (Yorkshire); Ullet (Cheshire); White-breasted Barn Owl; White Hoolet; White Owl (Surrey, Sussex, Worcester) Willow Owl (Surrey); Woolert (Shropshire); Yellow Owl.

BLUE TIT

BILLYBITER

PICKCHEESE

BLUE OX-EYE

BLUE TIT

It is not surprising that a bird which is so familiar to us should have such a wealth of folk-names. The **Blue Tit** is an energetic little acrobat whose antics in the garden delight us. Such antics include nibbling on the peanuts, or scolding aggressively from its nest (hence the term **Billy-biter**).

Many of its country names relate to its colourful plumage, especially the bright blue which is at its most vivid on the bird's head or cap. Hence **Blue Top**, **Blue Bonnet**, **Blue Mope** (mop) and all the rest. The terms **Nun** and **White Nun** relate to the band of white surrounding its crown, which is reminiscent of a nun's headgear. (The Smew is also called the **White Nun** on account of its similar black on white colouring).

The term **Ox-eye** was probably once widespread as a term used to denote any small thing (as in bull's eye). It has certainly been applied to other small birds such as the Treecreeper, and other members of the tit family. **Pickcheese** reflects the way in which Blue Tits would peck at a cheese in the same way as many now peck on milk-bottle tops. The Old English name for the Blue Tit was Hicemase (the old word hick meaning peck) and the term **Hickmall**, along with its other West Country corruption probably reflects this.

Allecampagne (Cornwall); ***Bee-bird (Hampshire);*** ***Betty Tit (Suffolk);*** ***Billy-biter (Sussex);*** ***Billy Pickcheese (Isle of Ely);*** ***Biting Tom (Northumberland);*** ***Bitter Tom;*** ***Black and Blue Titmouse;*** ***Blue-Bonnet (Ireland and Scotland);*** ***Blue Mope;*** ***Blue Ox-eye (Forfar);*** ***Blue Spick (Devon);*** ***Blue Thee;*** ***Blue Tit;*** ***Blue Tomtit;*** ***Blue Top;*** ***Blue Whaup;*** ***Blue Yaup (Scotland);*** ***Bluecap (Northumberland, Surrey);*** ***Bluey (Yorkshire);*** ***Hack, Hackymal, Hagmal, Hechymal, Hickmall (West Country);*** ***Jenny Tit (Suffolk);*** ***Jenny Wren (Yorkshire);*** ***Nun;*** ***Ox-eye (N England);*** ***Pedn-play, Pridden pal, (Cornwall);*** ***Pickatee (Nottinghamshire);*** ***Pickcheese (Norfolk, Suffolk);*** ***Pinchem (Bedfordshire);*** ***Stonechat (Ireland);*** ***Tidife;*** ***Tinnock;*** ***Titmal;*** ***Titmouse;*** ***Tittymouse, Tommy Titmouse (Somerset);*** ***Tom Nouf (Shropshire);*** ***Tom Nowp (Cheshire);*** ***Tom Tit;*** ***Whaup, Yaup (Scotland);*** ***White Nun;*** ***Willow Biter.***

DIPPER

WATER OUZEL

RIVER PIE

BESSIE DUCKER

DIPPER

The name **Dipper** could relate either to the bird's characteristic bobbing up and down on waterside stones (as does the term **Bobby**), or more probably its fascinating method of feeding by submerging itself completely in order to find aquatic insects under the stones on the river-bed. It is unique amongst songbirds in being able to walk under water like this. It is never seen away from the waterside, and not surprisingly, therefore, has the word "water" associated with many of its country names. Even the term **Ess Cock** has water at its heart, *ess* being a Scottish local word for waterfall from the Gaelic *eas*.

This attractive, rotund-looking bird frequents fast-moving upland streams and rivers. Its white bib and waistcoat contrasts starkly with the rest of its dark plumage. The terms **Colley** and **Water Colly** (meaning coaly or coal-like) are rather inaccurate however, as the Dipper is dark brown, chestnut and slate-grey. It is still often referred to as the **Water Ouzel**, the word *ouzel* or *ousel* being an archaic word simply for a blackbird. Its black appearance also lends it the Northern term **Water Crow**, and its contrasting plumage is further referenced in the names **River Pie** and **Piet**, the latter meaning either the noun *Magpie* or the adjective *pied*.

Bessie Doucker, Bessy Ducker (N England, S Scotland); **Bobby**; *Brook Ouzel; Colley (Cheshire); Didapper (Gloucestershire); Douk (Yorkshire); Ducker; Ess Cock (Scotland); Gobha Uisge [Water Smith] (Gaelic); Gobha Dhubh Nan Allt [Blacksmith of the Stream] (Gaelic); Kingfisher (Ireland, Scotland); Piet; River Pie (Ireland); Sand Thrush; Water Blackbird (Ireland, Scotland, Gloucestershire, Yorkshire); Water Colly (Somerset); Water Crake; Water Craw (N England); Water Crow (N England, S Scotland); Water Ouzel (Somerset); Water Peggy (Scotland); Water Piet; Water Piot; Water Pyet; Water Pyot; Water Thrush (Cornwall); Wetter-craw (Scotland); Willy Fisher (Yorkshire).*

GOLDCREST

MILLER'S • MILLER'S THUMB •

HERRING SPINK • HERRING

• KINGLET

GOLDCREST

As the smallest British bird, many of the folk names of the Goldcrest refer to its diminutive size: **Humming-bird**, **Little Wren**, **Thumb-bird**, **Tom Thumb** etc. Owing to its size, it is often heard before it is seen, making shrill little peeps amongst the highest boughs of its favoured conifer trees. The "tot" in the term **Tot O'er Seas** also adds this diminutive element, and the reference to over the sea relates to the migration of some Goldcrests. Flying to this country from Scandinavia, they would sometimes alight on the rigging of the North Sea herring boats in great flocks, from which habit they also earned the name of **Herring Spink**, literally "herring finch". Arriving in Britain at about the same time as migrating Woodcock gave it the name **Woodcock Pilot**. For such a small bird to travel such distances at all surprised people, and it was once thought that the Goldcrests hitched a lift on the back of Short-Eared Owls! (Overtones of another piece of small-bird folklore – "The Eagle and the Wren" whereby the Wren hitched a lift on the Eagle's back to win a flying competition and with it, the title "King of Birds".)

The Goldcrest's Latin name is **Regulus Regulus**, regulus being the diminutive form of rex, meaning king. It is clear from the golden crown on the Goldcrest's head why this name is appropriate, and other folk names reflect this royal connection: **Kinglet**, **Fire Crown**, and **Gold-crested Regulus**.

Copped Wren; *Fire Crown* (Yorkshire); *Gold-crested Kinglet*; *Gold-crested Regulus*; *Gold-crested Warbler*; *Golden-crested Wren*; *Golden Cutty* (Hampshire); *Golden Wren*; *Hawks-eye* (Somerset); *Herring Spink* (Suffolk); *Humming-bird*, *Jinny Wren*, *Kinglet*, *Little Wren* (Yorkshire); *Marigold Bird*; *Marigold Finch*; *Miller's Thumb*, *Moon*, *Moonie*, *Muin* (Scotland); *Sheely*, *Shiely* (Lindisfarne); *Swing Tree* (Suffolk); *Thumb-bird* (Hampshire); *Tidley Goldfinch* (Devon); *Tom Thumb* (Scotland); *Tot O'er Seas* (E England, Suffolk); *Wood Titmouse* (Cornwall); *Woodcock Pilot* (Yorkshire).

GREAT SPOTTED WOODPECKER

FRENCH PIE

MAGPIE-ILE

PIED WOODPECKER

GREAT SPOTTED WOODPECKER

The **Greater** Spotted Woodpecker became known as the **Great** Spotted Woodpecker after Thomas Pennant wrote his *British Zoology* in 1768. It is one of only three British Woodpeckers (Ireland has none), the other two being the Lesser Spotted Woodpecker and the Green Woodpecker. There is much folklore relating to woodpeckers, but the green, being at one time the most numerous British species of the three, has the most.

Many woodpecker legends have a connection with water – the terms **Rain Bird, Rain Fowl** and **Rain Pie** suggest that the bird was able to foretell rain. This was especially important to the woodpecker according to legend. In one version of the creation story, God had asked all of the birds to fly away and peck holes in order to make the earth's lakes and seas. Because the woodpeckers refused, not only were they condemned to peck wood for the rest of their days, but they were also denied the opportunity to drink from the lakes and rivers. They therefore had to wait for rain to satisfy their thirst.

Many names for woodpeckers relate to their arboreal habits, for example **Wood Knacker**, **Hew Hole**, or **Awl-bird**. The name **Hickwall** and its likely local corruptions **Ickwall**, **Eckle**, **Eequall**, and **Eeckle** probably derive from an old interpretation of the word *hick* meaning to peck. Other names relate to the Great Spotted's appearance: **Black and White Woodpecker, Pied Woodpecker, Magpie-ile** and **Wood Pie**. The term **French Pie** or **French Magpie** is applied to both spotted woodpeckers. It describes what were once regarded as the "foreign" woodpeckers simply because they were not the most prevalent species.

*Awl-bird; **Black and White Woodpecker** (Norfolk); **Eckle, Eeckle, Eequall, French Eecle, French Magpie, French Woodpecker** (Gloucestershire); **French Pie** (Leicestershire, S England); **Ickwall**; **Hew Hole**; **Hickwall** (Gloucestershire); **Hood-awl**; **Magpie-ile** (Gloucestershire); **Nickle**; **Pied Woodpecker** (Surrey); **Spickle Pied Woodpecker**; **Witwale**; **Witwall** (Gloucestershire); **Wood-awl**; **Wood Hack**; **Wood Knacker**; **Wood Pie** (Hampshire, Staffordshire, Surrey); **Wood Spack**; **Wood Sprite**; **Woodwale**; **Woodwall** (Hampshire).*

HOUSE SPARROW

GREY SPADGER

CUDDY

LUM LINTIE

HOUSE SPARROW

The name **House Sparrow** implies a long association between this species and human kind. Similarly the terms **Thatch** or **Thack Sparrow** tell of the bird's habit of nesting in our roofs. This is also the derivation of the names **Eaves Sparrow** and **Easing Sparrow**. (The word *easing* is a northern contraction of *eavesing*, relating to the word eaves as railing does to rail.) The Sparrow has suffered a significant population crash in recent years, but until then had been a ubiquitous feature of our towns and cities. Indeed, so prolific was it, that Sparrow eggs were once sold as an aphrodisiac! The bird's sometime pest status was reflected in the poem *Who Killed Cock Robin*, in which our subject was indeed the culprit.

The word **Sparrow** goes back to Old English *Spearwa*, and would at one time have been used for a variety of perching birds. (The name *Sparrow Hawk* reflects this more general usage rather than relating to a bird which preys exclusively on Sparrows.) Many of the folk names listed below are corruptions, contractions or diminutives of this original term. The name **Cuddy** is used as a term of endearment for many small creatures, and has also been applied to birds such as the Wren and Treecreeper. **Chissick** is probably an onomatopoeic interpretation of the Sparrow's chattering, whilst the origin of the Cumbrian **Craff** remains a complete mystery!

Brown Sparrow; *Chissick* (Somerset); *Collier* (Yorkshire); *Craff* (Cumbria); *Cuddy*, *Hoosie* (Northumberland); *Easing Sparrow* (Shropshire); *Eave Sparrow* (Nottinghamshire); *Grey Spadger* (Antrim); *Jim, Jim-jim* (Sussex); *Jit* (Cheshire); *Joey Spadger* (Hertfordshire); *Lum Lintie* (East Lothian); *Philip*; *Phip*; *Roo-doo, Row-dow* (Northamptonshire); *Snaddy, Snadger, Snurk* (Cheshire); *Spadge* (N England); *Spadger*; *Sparr, Sparrer* (Hertfordshire); *Speout, Speug, Sprig, Sprong, Sproug, Sprug, Spug, Spur, Spyng* (Northumberland, Scotland); *Spuggie, Spuggy* (Cumbria, Northumberland, Yorkshire); *Spurdie* (Scotland); *Spurk, Squadger* (Cheshire); *Starling* (Dunrossen); *Thack Sparrow, Thatch Sparrow* (Northamptonshire, Shropshire).

KESTREL

WINDHOVER

STONEGALL

MOUSE FALCON

KESTREL

Our most familiar falcon, the **Kestrel**'s common name goes back to Norman times. It is derived from the French *crécerelle* (rattle) and is an onomatopoeic reference to the bird's call. The much older English name **Stanniel** and its variations also makes reference to the Kestrel's call, deriving from the Old English *stangella* meaning literally *Stone Yeller*.

Kestrels will be familiar to most people as the *"motorway falcon"*. It is said to favour the motorway verges because the traffic's vibrations encourage prey species to show themselves. (The name *falcon* itself is likely to come from the Latin *falx* meaning sickle, reflecting the sickle shaped wings characteristic of the falcon genus.) Its characteristic hovering into the wind, always seeking to hold its head perfectly still, gives rise to many country names such as **Wind Fanner**, **Vanner Hawk**, **Willy Whip-the-wind** and **Windhover**.

In Medieval England different social classes were assigned their proper species of hawk with which to hunt. Barry Hines' novel *A Kestrel for a Knave* indicates the lowly designation of this common falcon. An old theory also held that the absence of Cuckoos in winter could be attributed to the fact that they turned into Kestrels and other hawks.

Blood Hawk (Somerset); Brown Hawk (Yorkshire); Castrel; Clamhan Ruadh [Red Kite] (Gaelic); Coystril; Creshawk (Cornwall); Cristel Hawk; Cudyll y Gwynt [Wind Hawk] (Wales); Fan Hawk, Fanner Hawk, Fleingall, Flutterer (Sussex); Field Hawk (Surrey); Hover Hawk (Buckinghamshire, Yorkshire); Jack Hawk (Cheshire); Kastril; Kechie, Kite (Shropshire); Keelie (Scotland); Kryssat (Cornwall); Little Red Hawk, Mouse Falcon, Mouse Hawk (Yorkshire); Maalin (Shetland); Red Hawk (Lancashire, Yorkshire, Scotland); Sparrow Hawk (Ireland, Kent, Sussex); Stanchel; Stand Hawk (Yorkshire); Stangall; Stannel Hawk; Stanniel; Steingall; Stone Hawk (Cheshire, Cornwall); Stonegall; Vanner Hawk (Sussex); Vuzzy Kite (Somerset); Willy Whip-the-wind; Wind Bivver, Wind Fanner (Sussex); Wind Hoverer (Suffolk); Windbibber (Kent, Sussex); Windcuffer (Orkney); Windhover (Somerset, Sussex); Windhover Hawk (Surrey, Sussex); Windsucker (Kent); Yellow-backed Hawk.

LITTLE GREBE

·TOM PUDDIN·

·BLACK CHIN·

·DRINKAPENNY·

LITTLE GREBE

This bird is one of few that has more than one name in general usage. The terms **Little Grebe** and **Dabchick** are both commonly used, referring to the bird's diminutive size. In the word Dabchick the prefix *dab* is probably a corruption of *dap*, meaning to bob and dip in the water (Isaac Walton in his *Complete Angler* of 1676 tells how to catch a chub by *daping* a grasshopper!).

Many other local names for the Little Grebe refer to its habit of diving. It is has been called simply **Diver**, or **Divedapper**, **Dive an' Dop**, **Divy Duck** and **Jack Douker**. The bird is also known as a **Spider Diver** and **Mole Diver**. It is a bird missed by many as it will dive at one's approach and surface amongst the reed cover, near which it invariably swims. The names **Black-chin or Black-chinned Grebe** clearly relate to its appearance, but less convincing are the terms by which the bird was known in Cheshire; **Arse-foot**, **Foot-arse** or **Foot-in-arse**. If you're shocked that the civilised folk of Cheshire could conceive of such titles it may help to know that the word arse was not regarded as vulgar until the seventeenth century!

Other names for the Dabchick reflect familiarity, such as **Rolling Pin**, **Drink-a-penny**, and in Cheshire **Tom Pudding** (on the occasions when they weren't being rude about its rump).

Arse-foot (Cheshire); Black-chinned Grebe (Berkshire); Bonnetie (Scotland); Dabber (Berkshire); Dabchick; Didapper; Diedipper; Dipchick (Somerset); Dipper, Dipper Duck (Yorkshire); Dive an' Dop (Norfolk); Dive Dapper (Ireland); Diver (Cheshire); Divy Duck (Norfolk); Dobber (Yorkshire); Dobchick (Suffolk); Dopper; Douker; Drink-a-penny (Lough Strangford); Ducker (Northumberland); Foot-arse, Foot-in-arse, Jack Diver, Little Diver (Cheshire); Jack Douker (Shropshire); Little Douker, Mither o' the Mawkins (Scotland); Mole Diver (Sussex); Peep o' Day (Yorkshire); Penny Bird (Ireland); Rolling Pin (Sussex); Small Arsfoot; Sma' Dooker (Northumberland); Small Douker (Scotland); Small Ducker (Yorkshire); Small Loon; Spider Diver (Sussex); Spog-ri-tom (Western Isles); Tom Pudding (Cheshire, Ireland, Shropshire, Yorkshire); Tom Puffin (Yorkshire); Wee Diver, Wee Douker (Scotland); Willy Hawkie (Ireland).

MAGPIE

CHATTERNAG

HAGGISTER

MAGGOT

MAGPIE

"One for sorrow, two for joy"; the opening of this familiar rhyme about the **Magpie** (there are many versions of subsequent lines) hints at the wealth of lore and mythology surrounding it. This is largely because of its black and white, or **Pie**d, plumage, which also earns it many related folk names. Black, of course, is associated with the devil - the Magpie according to one story was the only bird to refuse to enter the ark; another tale intimates that the birds have a drop of the devil's own blood in them! The Magpie's dry cackle, eerily human-like at times, reinforces the mythology and gives rise to many variations of the name **Chatternag**. The name **Haggister** also has this association, deriving from the Old High German *agalstra* meaning chatterer.

Mag is, of course, the diminutive of Margaret, which explains country names such as **Madge** and **Miggy**. The name **Magot Pie** was first recorded in Shakespeare's *Macbeth* and is said to derive from the French *Margot la Pie*. Subsequent names such as **Maggoty Pie** come from this. A further set of terms derive from the name *Agnes,* another familiar name applied to the Magpie. A pet form of *Agnes* was once commonly *Annot*. Append this to the prefix *pie* and names such as **Piannot** and **Pyanet** result. The more down-to-earth term **Egg Lift** refers to the Magpie's springtime predation on songbirds.

Bush Magpie; Chattermag (Surrey); Chatternag (Somerset); Chatterpie (Norfolk, Somerset, Staffordshire); Cornish Pheasant (Cornwall); Egg Lift (Lincolnshire); Haggister (Kent); Long-tailed Mag; Long-tailed Nan; Madge; Mag; Magget (Worcester); Maggie (Cheshire); Maggot (Gloucestershire); Maggoty Pie (Gloucestershire) Maggy (Northumberland); Magot Pie (E England, Midlands); Margaret's Crow; Margaret's Pie; Marget; Meggit; Miggy (N England); Mock-a-pie; Nan Piannot (Yorkshire); Nanpie (Lincolnshire, Yorkshire); Ninut (Nottinghamshire); Pianate (N England); Piannet, Piannot, (Cheshire); Pie; Pie Nanny (Yorkshire); Pied Margaret; Piet, Pinut, Piot (Cheshire); Pyanet, Pyenate (Northumberland); Pye Mag (Yorkshire); Pyet (Northumberland, Somerset); Tell-pie, Tell-pienot, Tell-piet (Yorkshire);

MISTLE THRUSH

· STORMCOCK ·

· MIZZLY DICK ·

SKRIKE

MISTLE THRUSH

Aristotle wrote that the **Mistle Thrush** "feeds on nought but mistletoe and gum". This name is probably a contraction of *Mistletoe Thrush*, but is often written as **Missel Thrush**. Its penchant for holly berries has similarly earned it names like **Holm Thrush** in the South West of England. It has the greatest number of folk-names of any British bird, rivalled only by the Hedge Sparrow, Chaffinch, Heron and Green Woodpecker. Many names refer to its harsh call - **Screech Drossle**, its large size (for a thrush) eg **Big Mavis**, or its habit of continuing to sing in bad weather - **Stormcock**. Some of its names, like **Jay**, **Grey Bird** and **Butcher Bird** (the Mistle Thrush is called **Shrike** because of its call) can be confusing as they are also given to other quite separate species. Its collective noun *mutation* derives from the ancient belief that at the age of about ten, the Mistle Thrush cast aside its old legs and grew new ones!

Bell-Throstle; *Big Felt* (Ireland)); *Big Mavis* (East Lothian); *Big Throstle* (N England); *Bull Thrush* (Hampshire); *Bunting Thrush*; *Butcher Bird* (Donegal); *Charcock* (N England); *Charlie Cock* (Yorkshire); *Corney Keevor* (Antrim); *Crakle*; *Don Felfoot,* (Suffolk); *Drassel Thrush* (Somerset); *English Fulfer* (Suffolk); *Felfit* (E Suffolk); *Feltie Flier* (Scotland); *Fendy-fare* (Ireland); *Fen Thrush* (Northamptonshire); *Fulfer* (Norfolk); *Hillan Piet* (Aberdeen); *Gawthrush* (Northamptonshire); *Golden Thrush* (Yorkshire); *Grey Bird* ((Somerset); *Hollin Cock* (Yorkshire); *Holm Thrush* (Cornwall); *Holm Cock* (Devon); *Holm Screech* (Dorset); *Horse Thrush* (Northamptonshire); *Jay* (N Ireland); *Jay Pie* (Wiltshire); *Jercock, Chercock* (Cumbria); *Jeremy Joy*; *Marble Thrush* (Northamptonshire); *Muzzel Thrush* (Roxburgh); *Mizzly Dick* (Northumberland); *Norman Gizer* (Oxfordshire); *Norman Thrush* (Craven); *Pickie* (Yorkshire); *Rattlethrush* (Yorkshire); *Sadcock* (Cheshire); *Saith, Screech* (Sussex); *Screech Drossle, Screech Thrush* (Gloucestershire); *Sedgecock, Settcock, Shell Cock, Shell Thrush, Shelly* (Cheshire); *Shrike*; *Skirlcock, Skirlock* (Derbyshire); *Skrike, Skrite* (South of England); *Snow Bird* (Gloucestershire); *Squawking Thrush* (Isle of Wight); *Stone Thrush* (Dorset); *Storm Bird, Storm Thrush, Stormcock* (Southern England); *Stercher, Stretch* (Gloucestershire); *Sycock,* (Derbyshire); *Thin Thresher, Thrice Cock* (Cheshire); *Throstle Cock* (Scotland); *Wood Thrush, Yellow Fulfar* (Scotland).

NIGHTJAR

GOAT SUCKER · FERN OWL · MOTH HAWK

NIGHTJAR

It is perhaps inevitable, but nevertheless sad, that a bird as beautiful as the **Nightjar** should have been associated with dark deeds, superstitions and names which it little deserves. Our fear of anything associated with the hours of darkness has bestowed on it such names as **Gabble Ratchet**, a reference to Gabriel Ratchet's Hounds - a pack of demon dogs that pursue the souls of the damned across the skies. (In Yorkshire the tale went that Nightjars were the lost souls of unbaptised infants!) It is called **Goatsucker** in Southern England because of an ancient belief that the bird sucked milk, vampire-like, from the udders of goats, leaving the animals sickly and poisoned. And it is unflatteringly referred to as **Flying Toad** in Lancashire and **Corpse Bird** (a term it shares with the Tawny Owl) in Cheshire.

It is in fact a bird of the night, its delicate, marbled plumage camouflaging it amongst the ferns and leaf-litter of the forest floor during the hours of daylight; hence **Fern Owl**, **Fern Hawk** and **Bracken Owl**. As darkness descends it begins its strange and haunting churring, a burbling call earning it names such as **Eve Churr**, **Heath Jar** and, rather unkindly, **Razor Grinder** and **Scissor Grinder**. Its long thin, hawk-like wings, nocturnal habits and insect diet give rise to many other self-explanatory names. **Puck Bird** is a reference to a hobgoblin or evil spirit (puck) and suggests that the **Nightjar** engages in similar mischievous activities as its namesake after dark !

Big Razor Grinder; *Bracken Owl (Cheshire)*; *Churn Owl (Northumberland)*; *Churr Owl (Scotland)*; *Corpse-bird (Cheshire)*; *Corpse-hound (Yorkshire)*; *Dew-fall Hawk*; *Dor-hawk (S England)*, *Doy-hawk (Suffolk)*; *Ejar (Surrey)*; *Eve Churr, Eve-jar (Hampshire, Sussex)*; *Evening Jar (Cheshire)*; *Fern Hawk (Gloucestershire)*; *Fern Owl*; *Flying Toad, Gabble Ratchet (Yorkshire)*; *Gnat Hawk (Hampshire)*; *Goat Chaffer (Scotland)*; *Goat Owl (Gloucester)*; *Goatsucker, Heath Jar, Heave Jar (Southern England)*; *Jar Owl*; *Jerry Spinner*; *Lich-fowl (Cheshire)*; *Moth Eater, Moth Hawk, Moth Hunter, Moth Owl*; *Night-churr, Night Crow (Cornwall)*; *Night Hawk*; *Night Owl, Night Swallow (Surrey)*; *Puck Bird, Puckeridge (Sussex)*; *Razor Grinder, Scissors Grinder (Norfolk)*; *Screech Hawk (Berkshire)*; *Spinner (Ireland)*; *Wheel Bird (Scotland)*; *Whip-poor-will (Gloucestershire)*.

NUTHATCH

JOBBIN

· BLUE WOODPECKER ·

· MUD-STOPPER ·

NUTHATCH

This delightful denizen of our older woodlands, looking like a masked bandit, has the reported distinction of being the only British bird able to walk whilst facing *down* the trunk of a tree. Although it will visit bird tables it is most at home amongst mature deciduous woods. It has been known, confusingly, simply as **Woodpecker**, and more helpfully as **Blue Woodpecker**, and **Blue Leg**.

The term **Nuthatch** probably developed from the more logical **Nut Hack** or **Nut Hacker**; this bird wedges nuts and acorns into cracks in the bark of a tree and hacks them open with its bill. It is therefore also known as the **Nutcracker** in Shropshire, not to be confused with the continental bird (a rare winter vagrant) of the same name. For similar reasons it is known too as the **Wood Cracker**, the **Nut Topper**, **Nut Tapper**, and in Surrey the **Woodhacker**.

The noun job can mean a sudden thrust with the beak, and as a verb the word can also mean to peck suddenly. Consequently the Nuthatch is called **Nut Jobber** in Sussex and **Jobbin** (sometimes spelt **Jobin**) in Northamptonshire.

The supposedly jarring sounds made by the feeding Nuthatch have earned it the names of **Jar Bird,** and in Gloucestershire the **Woodjar**, whilst its habit of reducing the size of its nest-hole by stopping it with mud has given rise to the names of **Mud Stopper** and **Mud Dabber** in Southern England.

Blue Leg (Sussex); Blue Woodpecker; Jar Bird; Jobbin (Northamptonshire); Mud Dabber, Mud Stopper (S England); Nut Tapper; Nut Topper; Nutcracker (Somerset, Sussex); Nut Hack; Nut Hacker; Nut Jobber (Somerset, Sussex); Wood Cracker; Wood Hacker (Surrey); Woodjar (Gloucestershire); Woodpecker (Surrey).

OYSTERCATCHER

·MUSSEL CRACKER· ·DICKIE BIRD·

KROCKET

OYSTERCATCHER

The unmistakable black and white plumage of the **Oystercatcher** with its great carrot bill gives rise to many of the bird's country names, as in **Pienet** or **Sea Pie** (its most common name until a hundred years ago). Interestingly some names derive from the word *sheld* which as well as having the meaning *variegated* or *particoloured* can also mean *pied*.

A faint sign of the cross is said to be seen on the Oystercatcher's breast as it flies, supposedly given to the bird after it hid Jesus from his enemies beside the Sea of Galilee. St Bride is said to have carried an Oystercatcher in each hand on her visit to Long Island, providing yet another religious association. This event gave the bird its names of **Gillie Bride**, **Bride's Page** and **St Bride's Lad**. In Saxon mythology the Oystercatcher is said to have been St Olaf's bird, and was thus given the name **Olive**. The name, however, is also said to be onomatopoeic, reflecting the distinctive piping call of the Oystercatcher. This is also the probable explanation for other of its folk names such as **Chaldrick** and **Tirma**. The names **Mussel Cracker** and **Mussel Pecker** reflect a more accurate description of its feeding habits than the term **Oystercatcher**; British birds almost certainly never catch oysters!

Bilcock (Wales); ***Bride's Page** (Hebrides);* ***Chalder, Chaldrick, Choldrick, (Orkney);* **Dickie Bird** *(Norfolk);* ***Gillie Bride, Krocket** (Scotland);* ***Mere-pie** (Suffolk);* ***Mussel Cracker** (N England);* ***Mussel Pecker** (Ireland, Scotland);* ***Olive** (Essex, Suffolk, Sussex);* ***Oyster Picker** (Somerset);* ***Oyster Plover;* **Pied Oyster Catcher**; **Pienet**; **Pynot** *(Northumberland);* ***Scolder** (Orkney);* ***Sea Magpie** (Gloucestershire); **Sea Nanpie** (Yorkshire);* ***Sea Pie** (Gloucestershire, Suffolk, Scotland);* ***Sea Piet** (Northumberland);* ***Sea Pilot; Sea Pyot** (Somerset);* ***Shalder, Shelder, Sheldro** (Shetland);* ***Skeldrake, Skeldro** (Orkney);* ***St. Bride's Lad** (Scotland);* ***Tirma, Tjalda** (Faero Isles);* ***Tirma, Trillachan, Trillichan** (Hebrides); **Trithcham**.*

PARTRIDGE

P. GREY BIRD

GIR GIRICK

STUMPEY

PARTRIDGE

Most folk names for this bird are either variations of the term **Partridge** or are descriptive of its appearance. The word partridge comes to us through various Norman (French) and Latin influences from the Greek *perdesthai* meaning "to make explosive noises"! Anyone who has disturbed this bird, which always seems reluctant to fly until the very last moment before imminent danger, will recognise the "explosive noise" reference. The term may also relate to the sometimes sudden, loud grating call of the Partridge.

The following names are rather bland descriptors of its actual plumage: **Brown Partridge**, **Grey Partridge**, **Nut-brown Bird**. Given its liking for farmland and field edges the Kentish term **Mountain Partridge** is even less accurate. At one time our **English Partridge** would have been the only partridge encountered in the British countryside, and therefore required only the simple name **Partridge** to define it. In the time of Charles II the Red-legged or French Partridge was introduced (quite possibly by the King himself to fill the parks at Windsor and Richmond). Although it is not certain whether these initial birds survived, further introductions certainly assured the British success of the species which is even more of a runner than our native bird. Subsequently it became necessary to have more defining names for our own **Common Partridge**.

A rather nice anecdote relating to the name of the Partridge suggests that the Middle English name *Pertriche*, because it sounds similar to "pear tree", gave rise to the association in the Christmas song *The Twelve Days of Christmas*. It's the best explanation so far of the rather uncharacteristic setting for a Partridge.

Brown Partridge; Common Partridge; English Partridge; Girgirick (Cornwall); Grey Bird (Suffolk); Grey Partridge; Grigear (Cornwall); Mountain Partridge (Kent); Nut-brown Bird; Pairtrick (Scotland); Partrick (Yorkshire); Pa'tridge (Hertfordshire); Partig, Partrig (Yorkshire); Patrick (Lancashire, Yorkshire, Scotland); Pertrick (Scotland); Stumpey (Sussex).

PUFFIN · SEA

PARROT

BILLED WILLY

MULLET

PARROT

PUFFIN

This bird's Irish name **Bill** rather sums it up! The characteristic broad, colourful beak gives rise to a number of names such as **Sea Parrot**, **Bottlenose**, **Knife Bill** and **Gulden Head**. Another beak-related term is **Coulter Neb**. A coulter is the wedge-shaped blade of a plough, whilst the word neb is another word for bill.

It's not just the bill though, which endears the **Puffin** to us. Its dumpy, upright stance, "black suit and white shirt" appearance and its facial expression all lend appeal. (The name **Tammie Norrie** was a term used in Orkney and Shetland for someone rather shy or doleful - the face and eyes of the puffin might explain its association). When blown about by gales these birds sometimes turn up in strange places, always cheering the observer and receiving attention disproportionate to the event. The attention was more deserved, no doubt, when one was found waddling along the Strand in 1935!

Some of the Puffin's names come from the places it frequents, hence **Ailsa Parrot** and **Bass Cock** (after Bass Rock). Conversely however, it is likely that Lundy Island was named after the birds which nested there - *lunde* is Icelandic for Puffin. Related names are **Lundi**, **Lunda**, and **Lunda Bouger**. The Gaelic terms **Bouger** and **Bulker** may be Norse in origin and mean "bird with the belly". Bless......

Ailsa Cock, Ailsa Parrot, Bass Cock (Scotland); Arctic Puffin; Barralot (Channel Isles); Bill (Ireland); Bottlenose (Wales); Bouger, Bulker (Hebrides); Bowger (St Kilda); Cockandy (Scotland); Coliaheen, Colisheen (Ireland); Coulter Neb (Northumberland, Sussex); Flamborough Head Pilot (Yorkshire); Gulden Head, Helegug (Wales); Knife Bill; Lunda; Lunda Bouger; Lundi (Fair Isles); Marrot; Mullet (Yorkshire); Norie (Shetland); Pal (Wales); Parrot (Yorkshire); Parrot-billed Will, Parrot-billed Wille, Parrot-billed Willcock, Parrot-billed Willy (Sussex); Pipe, Pope (Cornwall); Pisa[immature] (Fair Isle); Puffin of the Isle of Wight; Rockbird; Scout (Farne Islands); Sea Parrot (Norfolk, Northumberland, Sussex, Yorkshire); Tammie Norrie (Orkney, Shetland); Tom Noddy (Farne Islands); Tommody; Tommy; Willock (Kent).

RED-BACKED SHRIKE

BUTCHER BIRD · **NINE KILLER**

FLESHER

RED-BACKED SHRIKE

This handsome, chestnut-backed bird is a hook-beaked predator of small animals and large insects. Unfortunately it has declined significantly as a breeding species in this country, and is now more likely to be seen on migration.

The common name **Shrike** is also a folk name for the Mistle Thrush. The birds share a loud, harsh cry and the term relating to it comes from the Old English *scric*. The Shrike's fascinating habit of impaling its prey on nearby thorns earns it the names **Butcher Bird**, **Flesher** and their derivatives such as **Butcher Boy** and **Flusher**. **Murdering Pie** has similar origins. Only two Shrikes are seen in Britain with any regularity - this and the larger Great Grey Shrike, a winter visitor. Therefore the term **Lesser Butcher Bird** has also evolved for the Red-backed Shrike. The names **Nine Killer** and **Nine Murder** relate to an old country superstition that the Shrike would impale nine victims in its thorny larder before beginning to feed.

The German *wurger* and *wurchangel* (the latter meaning "destroying angel") gives rise to the names **Worrier** and **Wierangle** respectively. The Red-backed Shrike shares the name **Horse Match** with the Wheatear. Both birds have white on their rumps (although the Shrike's is on its tail and undertail coverts and not as pronounced) and the term is effectively a corruption. It started out as Hoar Smatch, literally *White Touch*. As the original usage of *hoar* became obsolete (except in the term *hoar frost*) so the name altered.

Butcher-bird; *Butcher Boy* (Surrey); *Cheeter* (Somerset, Sussex); *Common Flusher* (Surrey); *Cockoo's Maid* (Hereford); *Flesher*; *Flusher* (Yorkshire); *Flusher Shrike* (Surrey); *French Magpie, French Pie* (Sussex); *Granfer, Horse Jockey* (Somerset); *Horse Match* (Gloucestershire, Surrey); *Jack Baker* (Hampshire, Surrey, Sussex); *Lesser Butcher Bird*; *Mountain Magpie*; *Murdering Pie*; *Nine Killer*; *Nine Murder*; *Pope* (Hampshire); *Wierangle, Worrier* (N England); *Wurger* (Yorkshire).

RED-BREASTED MERGANSER

HERALD DUCK

SANDBILL

SPEAR WIGEON

RED-BREASTED MERGANSER

At one time known as the **Red-breasted *Goosander*, the Red Breasted Merganser** developed its now common name in 1752. It comes from the Latin *merg* meaning diving and *anser* meaning goose. The Merganser is one of a number of birds, including the Goosander and Smew, referred to as **Saw-bill**s because of the serrated edge to their fish-catching bills. The Red-breasted Merganser's sharp, thin bill also gives rise to further names such as **Spear Drake** and **Spear Wigeon**. In addition, its fishing habits earn the bird names such as **Diving Duck** and **Lesser Toothed Diver**. (The term *lesser* distinguishes the Merganser from the slightly larger toothed diver, the Goosander.)

The Red-Breasted Merganser is as much a bird of salt water as of fresh, often frequenting estuaries and northern sea lochs. It has a somewhat "scruffy ruffian" appearance in contrast to the sleeker Goosander, although the females of both species resemble each other to a much greater extent than the males. These duller females with their grey backs and reddish-brown heads earn them the names **Dun** and **Lesser Dun Diver**.

The name **Herald Duck** and its derivatives stem from the Icelandic word for duck - *haveld*. (The misspelling *hareld* is also the name for the Long-tailed Duck), whilst the French for Merganser – **Harle** gives rise to names like **Land Harlan**, **Herle**, and **Earl Duck**.

Bardrake; Diving Duck; Dun Diver [immature & female] (Yorkshire); Earl Duck, Goone, Grey Diver, (Scotland); Harle (Orkney); Herald, Herald Duck (Orkney, Shetland); Herl, Herle (Northumberland); Land Harlan (Ireland); Lesser Dun Diver [female]; Lesser Toothed Diver; Popping Wigeon (Ireland); Rodge; Sandbill (Sussex); Saw-neb (Scotland); Saw-bill (Scotland, Sussex, Yorkshire); Sawbill Daver (Suffolk); Sawbill Duck (Sussex, Yorkshire); Sawbill Wigeon (Ireland); Sawyer (Suffolk); Serula; Spear Drake, Spear Duck (Sussex); Spear Wigeon (Ireland); Tuke, Whistler (Sussex); Yarrell, Yearal, Yearel (Northumberland).

RED KITE

GREEDY GLED · PUTTOCK · CROTCH-TAIL ·

RED KITE

Another conservation success story, the **Red Kite** is now firmly established in what was once its last precarious foothold in Wales. In addition, release programmes in England and Scotland are proving successful in promoting the widespread population of this wonderful bird.

One of the bird's defining characteristics compared to the non-native Black Kite is its more deeply forked, reddish tail. It uses this with eye-catching effect as it manipulates the air currents in spectacular flight. Hence the names **Fork-tail**, **Crotch-tail** and **Swallow-tailed Falcon**. The Kite uses its wings sparingly, and its frequent gliding action gives rise to one of its oldest names - **Glead**. With references to Old English *glida* the word means simply Glider, and has many derivatives and corruptions as listed below. (**Greedy Gled** relates to its greedy scavenging amongst the once insanitary streets of towns and cities in bygone times.) Now, of course, the word *kite* is also used for the "flying" toy that owes its name to the similar hanging motion of this bird in the air. The Kite's sweeping flight is also encapsulated in the names **Puttock** and **Puddock**, the words being derived from Old English roots and meaning "Swooper".

The latter term is shared with the Buzzard, and indeed the words *Buzzard* and *Kite* are often interchanged in their use (erroneously) as generic terms for large birds of prey. The name **Bald Kite** has also been applied to the Buzzard, but it would seem more appropriate for the Red Kite, whose whitish head might well appear bald from a distance.

Baegez, Bargez (Cornwall); Bald Kite; Barcud, Bascud, Bascutan, Bod, Bodfforchog (Wales); Crotch-tail (Essex); Crotchet-tailed Puttock; Fork-tail (Yorkshire); Fork-tailed Kite; Forked Kite; Forky-tailed Kite, Glead (Sussex); Glead Hawk (Cheshire); Gled; Gledd; Glede; Glen Tanner Glead; Greedy Gled (N England, Scotland); Kyte; Puddock; Puttock; Red Glead; Red Kite; Salmon-tailed Glead; Scoul (Cornwall); Swallow-tailed Falcon.

RED-THROATED DIVER

SILVER GREBE

RAINGOOSE

COBBLE

RED-THROATED DIVER

This bird's alternative names of **Speckled Diver** or **Speckled Loon** (the latter shared with Black-throated diver) relate to its appearance and are self explanatory. In Norfolk it is the **Mag Loon** (the word *mag* meaning magpie) and in Suffolk the **Sprat Loon.** The word **Loon** is often synonymous with divers. As well as being the standard term in North America for the Great Northern Diver, loon is also an element of various folk names for *all* divers. The word literally means "fool", and is sometimes also applied to the Great Crested Grebe. However, "loon" may also be linked to the diver's haunting cry, as the word for red-throated diver in old Norse also means moan. Interpreted as a roar in Ireland, the diver's cry also gives rise to the name **Burrian**, translated in the Gealic as "roarer".

Divers have both a romantic and a mythological quality about them. They frequent wilderness areas and certainly in Britain are associated with the romance of the Highlands of Scotland. The red-throated diver nests here on remote lochans, carrying its young on its back. The mythology surrounding divers often relates to their human-like wailing cry; the birds were once thought to accompany the souls of the dead. The cry of the **Rain Goose** was also said to foretell rain. An immature red-throated diver is known as a **Cobble.**

Arran ake (Scotland); **Burrian** *(Ireland);* **Canadian Diver; Cobble; Dun Diver, Herring-bar** *(Sussex);* **Galrush** *(Ireland);* **Guinea-bird Diver** *(Yorkshire);* **Kakera;** *Leaan (Yorkshire)* **Little Lyon, Little Nack** *(Northumberland);* **Lune, Loon,** *(Devon, Cork, Orkney);* **Loom** *(Shetland);* **Mag Loon** *(Norfolk);* **Rain Goose** *(Orkney,Shetland);* **Red-necked Diver; Red-throated Loon; Sheep's-Head-and Pluck** *(Yorkshire);* **Silver Grebe** *(Kent);* **Speckled Diver; Speckled Loon, Sprat Borer, Sprat Loon** *(Essex);* **Spratoon** *(Norfolk, East Lothian).*

RINGED PLOVER

SANDY LOO

WIDE AWAKE

• BULL'S EYE

RINGED PLOVER

The **Ringed Plover** is a bird of the coast, "ring" appertaining to its black collar, hence **Ring-neck**, **Ring Dotterel** and **Ringlestone**. The penetrating call common to this family of birds was translated as the word *plo*. Thus **Plover** is to *plo* as whistler is to whistle. The Norse folk, however deciphered this bird's call as *lo*, giving rise to names such as **Sandy Loo**. An attempt to render the somewhat musical call is also witnessed in the names **Tranillys**, **Tullet** or **Tullot**, **Dulwilly** and **Wideawake**.

The Ringed Plover's habitat features in many of its country names. **Sand Snipe**, **Sand Tripper**, **Stone Runner**, **Sea Dotterel**, **Shell Turner** etc.. Within these surroundings the bird can camouflage itself completely - seeming to emerge from nowhere on a stony beach. This characteristic no doubt, gave rise to the name **Stonehatch**. So well disguised is it that it has learned to run and sit still rather than fly as a means of defence. This inclination to stay on the ground, where it blends in so well, has earned it the name of groundling or **Grundling** as it is written.

The word *laverock* in the names **Land Laverock** and **Sandy Laverock** is an old equivalent word for lark, widespread in the north, and stems from the Old English *laferce*.

Alexandrine Plover; **Bull's Eye** *(Ireland)*; **Dulwilly**; **Grundling** *(Lancashire)*; **Knot** *(Ireland)*; **Land Laverock** *(Scotland)*; **Martin Dotterel** *(Sussex)*; **Ring Dotterel**; **Ring-neck** *(Yorkshire)*; **Ringed Dotterel** *(Sussex, S Scotland)*; **Ringlestone**; **Sand Dotterel** *(Suffolk, Yorkshire)*; **Sand Lark** *(Northumberland, Sussex)*; **Sand Plover**; **Sand Runner** *(E Yorkshire)*; **Sand Snipe**; **Sand Tripper** *(County Down)*; **Sandy** *(Northumberland)*; **Sandy Laverock** *(Northumberland, Orkney, Shetland)*; **Sandy Loo** *(Orkney, Shetland)*; **Sandy Loog** *(Dunrossness)*; **Sea Dotterel**; **Sea Lark**; **Shell Turner**, **Shultener** *(Sussex)*; **Stone Plover**; **Stone Runner** *(Norfolk, Suffolk, Sussex)*; **Stonehatch** *(Suffolk)*; **Tranillys**; **Tullet**, **Tullot** *(Cheshire, Lancashire)*; **Wideawake** *(Somerset)*.

ROBIN

·RED BELLY·

·TOMMY-LIDEN·

·RUDDOCK

ROBIN

The name **Robin** is a diminutive of Robert and has only been attributed to a bird comparatively recently. Prior to the 1950s **Redbreast** was its common name and is still in widespread use today, either by itself, or as its extension of **Robin Redbreast**. The terms **Robinet** and **Robeen** are further examples of how this core name has differed in both place and time. The term **Ruddock** is an Anglo Saxon one. Like most other names for this bird, it also refers to the ruddy breast of the Robin.

We have a tradition of admiring our Robins - Robin Hood and Robin Adair being two of our folk heroes - so perhaps the familiar name demonstrates how we treasure this little bird. One piece of mythology states that to harm a Robin is to bring ill-fortune upon oneself. This may have been believed - at a time when many other songbirds were being caged or eaten, it seems the Robin escaped attention. It seems also, however, to have escaped the attention of the local name-givers. That a bird so endearing and so familiar to us should have such relatively few folk names is rather surprising.

The Robin is thought by many to be our National Bird, but this privilege is reserved for the wren, with whom the Robin shares a number of folk tales. One such is the tale of how, in bringing human kind the gift of fire, the Robin held the fire too close resulting in its characteristic red breast. (In some variations it is the wren which the brings the fire.)

Bob (Nottinghamshire); **Bob Robin**, (Somerset, Surrey); **Bobby** (Somerset); **Broindergh** [Red Belly] (Gaelic); **Ploughman's Bird** (Yorkshire); **Redbreast**; **Reddock** (Dorset); **Robeen**; **Robin Redbreast**; **Robin Ruck** (N England); **Robinet**; **Ruddock** (Cornwall, N. England); **Thomas Gierdet**; **Tommy-liden**; **White Robin** [when the eggs it lays are white] (Cheshire); **Yr Hobel Goc** [Red Bird] (Wales).

STONECHAT

FURZE HACKER

GORSE JACK

MORETETTER

STONECHAT

The fact that the **Stonechat** had the folk names **Bullfinch** and **Blackcap** serves only to support the arguments for standardisation across avian nomenclature. Where these were used, it leads one to consider what the commonly applied names for the actual Bullfinch and Blackcap used to be. The Stonechat's black head finds its way into many other of its names, including the splendid **Black Head of Gorse**, which sounds rather like a member of the nobility in times gone by!

The name Stonechat is, of course, descriptive of its chattering sound, much like two pebbles or stones being knocked together. (In a further confusion the term was originally applied to the Wheatear.) Many of its other country names are variations on this theme, for example **Stone Clink**, **Chickstone** and **Furze Chitter**. The term **Winter Utick**, like many others, is shared with the bird's similar cousin, the Whinchat. Utick is intended also to be an onomatopoeic rendition of the Stonechat's call, although the prefix of **Winter** for this bird is not so easily explained.

The preferred moor and heathland habitat of the Stonechat is mirrored in other names: **Moor Tit**, **Heath Jack** etc.. The bush commonly found in these settings also has its own alternative names: gorse, whin, and furze. These names in turn appear in **Gorse Chat**, **Whin Bird**, **Furze Jack** and others. Although mainly insectivorous, the **Blackberry Eater** will indeed also eat berries.

Black Head of Gorse; Black-headed Bank-chat; Black-headed Bushchat; Black-headed Furzechat; Blackberry Eater; Blackcap (Gloucestershire, Somerset); Blacky Cap (Ireland); Blacky Top; Bullfinch (Sussex); Bushchat; Chickstone (Yorkshire); Furze Chat (Suffolk); Furze Chitter, Furze Clitter (Cornwall); Furze Hacker (Hampshire); Furze Hackle, Furze Jack, Fuzz-Chat, Fuzz Jack (Sussex); Fuz Clacker (Surrey); Gorse Chat, Gorse Jack (Gloucestershire); Hawth Tit, Heath Jack, Heath Tit (Sussex); Moor Tit, Moor Titling, Red-breasted Moor Tit, Moretetter (Yorkshire); Stanechacker (Scotland, Yorkshire); Stane Chapper; Stone Chucker (Sussex); Stone Clink; Stone Smich; Stone Smith; Stonechatter (Sussex); Stoneclick; Stone Clocharet (Forfar); Stoneprick, Stonepricker (Cheshire); Sweep Jack (Sussex); Vuzzy Napper (Somerset); Wall Chat; Whin Bird (Suffolk); Winter Utick (Cheshire).

WATER RAIL

·GVTTER COCK·

·RAT HEN·

·BROOK OUZEL·

WATER RAIL

The **Water Rail** is so defined in order to distinguish it from the Land Rail or Corncrake. This was not its traditional name but one which was adopted in the seventeenth century. The name **Bilcock** (a term shared with the Moorhen as is the name **Moorhen** itself) is likely to be older and is a corruption of *biltcock*. This in turn comes from the Middle English *bulten* meaning to run quickly or to bolt. This refers to the Water Rail's preferred method of running to safety when disturbed rather than flying. This is echoed in the names **Brook Runner**, **Jack Runner** and **Velvet Runner**. Further descriptions of this bird's behaviour are found in the Lancashire term **Scarrigrise** meaning scared-in-the-grass, as well as in **Skitty**, **Skitty Coot** and **Skitty Cock** where skit means to dart or run quickly.

The Water Rail is a shy, retiring bird often affording only a fleeting glimpse to the observer. Within such a context, the descriptive terms of **Brown Hen** or **Grey Skit** may well be reasonable. However, they do not do justice to the plumage colouration and contrasting red beak when viewed more closely. Water Rails are certainly not black, and the term **Brook Ouzel** seems inappropriate (ouzel meaning *blackbird*). This term is also more accurately applied to the Dipper, and it may simply be that a mistake was made when the name was first written in 1678. The strange grunting call of the Water Rail is called groaning or **Sharming**; the latter has been adopted in Norfolk as its country name.

Bilcock (Yorkshire); Brook Ouzel; Brook Runner; Brown Hen; Common Rail; Darcock; Grey Skit (Devon); Greyhen; Gutter Cock (Cornwall); Jack Runner (Gloucestershire); Moorhen; Oar Cock; Rail (Suffolk); Rat-bird, Rat Hen, Runner (Yorkshire); Scarragrise (Lancashire); Sharming (Norfolk); Skitty, Skitty Cock, Skitty Coot (Cornwall, Devon, Somerset); Velvet Runner; War Cock; Water Hen (Ireland).

YELLOW WAGTAIL

·DISHWASHER·

·OATSEED BIRD·

·MAW-DAW

YELLOW WAGTAIL

It is easy to see why **Sunshine Bird** is an alternative name for the **Yellow Wagtail**. The most colourful of Britain's regularly-seen wagtails, it is not only the bird's yellow plumage which earns it this name but also its status as a Summer migrant - hence the names **Spring Wagtail** and **Summer Wagtail**. However, the mention of seeds in some of its names also refers to the bird's arrival in spring, or seed-time. Thus **Barley Bird**, **Oatseed Bird** and **Potato Dropper** are not related to the birds feeding behaviour (the Yellow Wagtail is insectivorous), but rather to its season. It is called names like **Cow Klit** because it is often seen pecking at insects amongst cattle. The word *klit* relates to the clicking sound made as it snaps at a fly.

The Yellow Wagtail shares many of its names with other wagtail species. This is certainly true of the name **Dishwasher** and associated terms, the birds' bobbing movements and tail-wagging sharing a common motion with the action of scrubbing dishes. As everyone reading this will know, dishwashing was once the exclusive domain of the female, (now much more balanced, no doubt!) hence further names for this bird of **Lady Dishwasher** and **Ladybird**. There is also an echo perhaps, of a certain feminine grace in the Yellow Wagtail's appearance and movements. The names **Yellow Molly** and **Bessy Blakeling** continue the female association. The Old Norse word *bleikr* meaning yellow gives rise to the word blakeling. Perhaps unsurprisingly, Bessy Blakeling is also a name associated with the Yellowhammer.

Barley Bird (Nottinghamshire, Surrey, Sussex); Barley-seed Bird (Yorkshire); Bessy Blakeling; Cow-bird (Sussex); Cow Klit; Cow Kloot; Dishwasher (Sussex); Golden Dishwasher (Somerset); Lady Dishwasher (Gloucestershire); Ladybird, Maw Daw (Sussex); Oat Ear; Oatseed Bird; Potato Dropper, Potato Setter, Tater-setter (Cheshire); Quaketail; Ray's Wagtail; Spring Wagtail; Summer Wagtail; Sunshine Bird; Yellow Molly (Hampshire); Yellow Waggie.

The list of folk names for all of the British Birds is too extensive to print here. However, readers wishing to access a comprehensive list will be able to do so from those books identified by an asterisk within the following bibliography.

BIBLIOGRAPHY

Bosworth Smith, R	*Bird Life and Bird Lore*	John Murray, 1905
Brown, W J	*The Gods Had Wings*	Constable & Company Ltd, 1936
Hare, C E	*Bird Lore*	Country Life Ltd., 1952
Jackson, Christine E	*British Names of Birds**	H.F.&G Witherby Ltd., 1968
Greenoak, Francesca	*All the Birds of the Air**	André Deutsch Ltd., 1979
Lockwood, W B	*The Oxford Dictionary of British Bird Names**	Oxford University Press, 1984
Lodge, Walter	*Birds Alternative Names, A World Checklist*	Blandford, 1991
Addison, Josephine & Hillhouse, Cherry	*Treasury of Bird Lore*	André Deutsch Ltd., 1998